Find Your Funny

The Humor Survival Guide

—⁂—

BARB BEST AND JOANNE JACKAL PHD

Find Your Funny: The Humor Survival Guide
Copyright © 2016 Barb Best and Joanne Jackal PhD
2nd Edition 2018

BBevHills Publishing, Los Angeles, CA

All rights reserved.

No part of this book may be reproduced or transmitted in any form or by any means, electronic or mechanical, including photocopying, recording or by any information storage and retrieval system, without written permission from the authors, except for the inclusion of brief quotations in a review.

Cover Design: Katrina Joyner
Interior Design: Kim Morehead
Illustration Credits: iStock.com

ISBN: 978-1-7323181-0-6

FIND YOUR FUNNY: The Humor Survival Guide
SERIOUSLY!

"This book is a "must read" for every teenager who wants to put more fun and laughter into their life. It is incredibly funny and enormously practical at the same time. This gem of a book can truly change the world by sharing with teens the joyful gift of laughter and by empowering them to develop humor as a vital coping skill. This book has my highest recommendation as a resource for teens, tweens and for adults who are young at heart."

–**Mary Kay Morrison** President, AATH: Association of Applied and Therapeutic Humor; Founder: Humor Quest; Author: *Using Humor To Maximize Living: Connecting with Humor*

"I've never read a better, more informative volume on the value of humor and laughter. **FIND YOUR FUNNY** can now be considered the quintessential book on the importance of humor in our lives. (I wish I had written it.)"

–**Larry Wilde** The NY Times bestselling author of *How The Great Comedy Writers Create Laughter and Great Comedians Talk About Comedy*

"The Activities are creative and playful. The Information is amusing and transformative. This isn't a "Have To" Book. This is a "Want To" Book."

–**Jim Winter** Educator, Humorist Founder & President of Wavelength Inc: the global touring improvisational ensemble of actors and educators

"***Find Your Funny: The Humor Survival Guide*** is packed with laughter fun-facts and practical tips on how to flex your humor muscles. One of the most important aspects of this book is the support the authors provide to help teens cope with and manage negative emotions."

–**Christa Scalies** Founder, *Giggle On*®, Advocate for laughter as a wellness tool for improved mental, spiritual, physical and emotional health and author of *Suicide Sucks*

"I wish I had this book when I was younger. It's fun, uplifting, and positive. And I love the Cool Comedy Pages in the middle."

–**Suzanne Raga** Author of *YOU ROCK! How To Be A Star Student & Still Have Fun!*

"Today's teens surely need to find and use their funny bones! They need to know how helpful their sense of humour can be in stress-filled lives – both their lives and their friends' lives. **Find Your Funny: The Survival Guide** is packed with strategies for teens to use to make it through those times when laughter seems too far off their radar screen."

> –**Sue Stephenson**, Speaker and author of *Kidding Around: Connecting Kids with Happiness, Laughter and Humour*

CONTENTS

Just Kidding!..xi

Introduction: Why Develop a
Great Sense of Humor?......................xiii

Chapter 1   Your New BFF...............................1

                Physical Benefits of Humor
                and Laughter..2

                Psychological Benefits of Humor
                and Laughter..4

                Social Benefits of Humor
                and Laughter..6

Chapter 2   "Got Laughter?" Quiz:
                Test Your Humor Level!........................9

                Scoring...13

Chapter 3	What Makes you Laugh?............................15	
Chapter 4	How to be a Humor Sponge......................26	
	Top Ten Ways to Find your Funny..........35	
	You're so Funny!!! ☺ Cool Comedy Pages ☺........................37	
Chapter 5	Sharing the Funny......................................49	
	Sharing is Caring....................................51	
Chapter 6	Going the Extra Smile................................55	
	More Ideas to Flex your Humor Muscle:..56	
	Top Seven Ways to Find More of your Funny!..60	

Chapter 7	Lights…Camera…Laughter	62
	Five Comedy Improv Exercises	63
Chapter 8	Humor & Happiness	67
	Seven Easy Steps	71
	How not to be ☺	76
Chapter 9	Good Humor Gone Bad	77
	Yays	77
	Nays	78
	Humor And Bullies	79
	Tips	80
	Gender Differences: He Laughed / She Laughed	82

| Chapter 10 | You've Got to be Kidding | 87 |

Fun Facts about Laughter and Jokes........87

Resources Comedy 411..................................97

Funny Stuff Is Out There! Find Your Funny!..97

Comedy Movies.......................99

Resources Tragedy 411..................................102

Hotlines...................................103

More Help! Go Online..........................104

About The Authors..107

Acknowledgments..109

JUST KIDDING!

"This book is freakin' better than a spin in my baby-blue Ferrari." –Justin Bieber

"I fell wildly in love with this book. I'm writing a hit song about it." –Taylor Swift

"Everything I know about comedy is in this dumb book." –Adam Sandler

"Four out of five zombies dig *Find Your Funny*." –Google

"This book will make you healthy, wealthy and funny." –Benjamin Franklin

"More fun than a bikini wax. Check it out!" –Lucy Hale

"This book rocks. It's SEXY! Gobble it up, guys."
–Ashton Kutcher

"Ask not what your funny bone can do for you; ask what you can do for your funny bone." –John F. Kennedy

Find Your Funny is like totally crazy… and I know crazy." –Lady Gaga

"Better than twerking in your thong on live TV!"
–Miley Cyrus

"The second best book of all time!" –Jesus Christ

"Just eat it! Grab a fork and read it!" –Weird Al

"I'm studying *Find Your Funny* to get my funny back."
–Mom

"Read this book and have more friends…like me!"
–Class Clown

INTRODUCTION

WHY DEVELOP A GREAT SENSE OF HUMOR?

> "The most wasted of all days is one without laughter."
> – e . e . cummings

Do you enjoy comedy? Do you like to laugh? Would you like to laugh more? This book will show you how to increase the level of fun and happiness in your life by sharpening your humor skills. You will discover how to find the funny both in your world and, more importantly, in yourself. You will learn how to use humor to deal with stressful and difficult situations. Did you know that humor is a cool power tool that can help zap negative thoughts, behaviors and attitudes?

Why should you care about having more humor and laughter in your life? Good question. Developing a robust sense of humor is an important part of creating and sustaining happiness. Happiness feels good, so much better than being miserable. Smiling beats crying. Rocking with laughter is preferable to rolling on the floor blubbering.

Guess what? Research shows that laughter, humor and happiness have a positive effect on your physical, psychological and emotional health. Humor helps you connect socially. It helps you make friends and get along better with the ones you already have. And it's a great way to de-escalate a tense situation. Maybe you've even used it to get your parents to chill when they're up in your grill about something. Wouldn't it be great to see the humor in really annoying situations instead of losing it?

Finding your funny won't make all your problems disappear, but developing humor skills will help you cope with difficult times in your life. Don't worry—it's not about making you into someone who fakes being happy all the time.

Negative emotions are normal and appropriate in many situations. If you can learn to manage them more successfully, you will be happier and have more fun ... and if you are happier and having more fun, you will cope with your negative emotions and difficult problems more effectively. It's a positive feedback loop, a virtuous circle, a self-fulfilling prophecy, and a heck of a lot better than running in circles like a caged rat on a treadmill. Whew!

Find Your Funny will empower you by increasing your competence in a vital life skill–humor. It's as important as healthy eating, exercise, sleep and texting under the table. Free yourself to be playful and have fun. Loosen up. Get silly. Slip and slide out of your comfort zone. You will not only find your funny; you will build emotional muscle and strengthen your funny bone. Here's to laughter!

ONE
YOUR NEW BFF

> "The human race has one really effective weapon, and that is laughter."
> – Mark Twain

Humor is a friend with healthy benefits – physical, psychological and social. There is even a field of study called **gelotology** from the Greek *gelos* meaning laughter. It's the study of laughter and its effects on the body, from a psychological and physiological perspective.

The research will amaze you. Here's what it shows.

Physical Benefits of Humor and Laughter

- Is your thinking a little sluggish? Laughter helps you think better. It improves your breathing, and that increases oxygen in the blood. The oxygen in the blood is carried to the brain and that wakes up your thinking.

- Need a workout? Laughter has been called "inner jogging" by stress relief expert David S. Sobel, MD. While you're laughing, the muscles in your abdomen, shoulders, face and diaphragm get a good workout. Your blood pressure and heart rate go up temporarily and your breathing becomes deeper, increasing the oxygen in your blood. When you stop laughing, your muscles relax deeply and your heart rate and blood pressure decrease. The harder you laugh, the bigger the decrease in tension and the longer it lasts.

- Feeling stressed? Laughter leads to a reduction in stress hormones that constrict blood vessels and suppress immune activity. Medical researcher Lee Berk, PhD, points out this effect lasts for about 30 minutes after your "laugh attack."

- In other words, in addition to decreasing your stress, laughter might also help you fight off illness.

- Laughter protects the heart. Positive psychology expert Barbara L. Fredrickson, PhD, has found that people who cannot laugh or smile in an uncomfortable or stressful situation are more likely develop heart disease. People with a history of heart disease are more likely to get hostile or angry rather than use humor to overcome the embarrassment or stress of a situation.

- Need some energy? The increased oxygen in your blood that wakes up your brain also energizes your body. It improves circulation to your heart, lungs, adrenal glands and digestive system.

- Where does it hurt? Laughter reduces pain. It does this in two ways. First, it's a great distraction from your pain. It takes your mind off it for a while. Second, laughter may cause one of the body's natural painkillers, endorphins, to be produced and released into the blood system.

- Laughter lowers blood pressure. "Not me! I'm too young!" Yes, you! Blood pressure in American teens is on the rise due to lack of exercise, obesity and diets high in salt. High blood pressure can lead to cardiovascular disease later in life. So, drop those chips, go for a jog, and have a good laugh.

- Just say no! You don't need harmful drugs, because laughter does the same thing. Well, almost! Humor activates brain networks that are involved in rewards. This is the same brain network that is activated by drugs like marijuana, ecstasy and cocaine. Laughter makes us feel good. We feel rewarded. And it's free and legal!

Psychological Benefits of Humor and Laughter

- Humor improves mood and decreases negative emotions. It's hard to feel depressed when you're laughing. Humor keeps us from being overly serious about our problems. It helps us fight pessimistic thinking. According to the April 2013 issue of *Good Housekeeping* magazine, "A study at The University of Luxembourg found that if you laugh gently at a misstep instead of belittling yourself, you'll be less tense and feel a greater sense of well-being."

- Humor is a coping mechanism. This is a big one! When we are able to joke about our problems and make fun of ourselves, difficult situations don't seem so overwhelming. We are able to create some distance and perspective. This provides us with an emotional (whoopee) cushion to soften the pain.

When we use humor to cope with a problem, we are changing our way of thinking about it. This leads to a shift in how we feel about the situation. Instead of feeling helpless and hopeless, we feel a sense of control and power over the problem.

The most remarkable use of humor as a coping mechanism comes from interviews of people who survived the Holocaust. How is it possible that they found any humor in their desperate situation? Here's what survivors told Holocaust researcher Chaya Ostrower, PhD:

> "Look, without humor we would all have committed suicide. We made fun of everything. What I'm actually saying is that that helped us remain human, even under hard conditions ... But don't think that it is possible for people in such situations *not* to have any humor and satire. This is impossible; it is a kind of defense mechanism ..."

The use of humor by the prisoners of the

Holocaust did not reduce the actual horror of their situation; it did help them remain mentally strong and survive.

It's safe to say that none of us will ever have to endure anything close to the pain, despair and terror that these Holocaust survivors endured. Let's be inspired and guided by their strength and wisdom. If they could use humor to make their situation bearable, surely we can learn to use it to help us cope in our lives.

Life Is Beautiful is a great film about a man who uses humor to help his family survive during their internment in a Nazi concentration camp.

Social Benefits of Humor and Laughter

- Humor helps us attract and maintain close relationships. A sense of humor is something we look for in friends. We appreciate it when someone can diffuse a tense situation with humor.

- Humor enhances relationships. We like to laugh. Our brain rewards us for laughing. We like to be with people who make us laugh.

Find Your Funny

- Laughter is a very social behavior. We laugh 30 times more when we're with people than when we're alone, according to neuroscientist and psychology professor Robert R. Provine.

- Laughter leads to social bonding. In fact, many researchers believe that this is the purpose of laughter.

- The more we relax and laugh with people, the more bonding there is. And the more bonding there is, the more we laugh.

> "The ability to laugh at oneself when faced with events beyond one's control, to admit to blunders with humor, and to find humor in all situations is a critical life skill."
> **– Mary Kay Morrison,**
> *Using Humor to Maximize Living*

> "Life is tough, and if you have the ability to laugh at it, you have the ability to enjoy it."
> **– Salma Hayek**

TWO
"GOT LAUGHTER?" QUIZ: TEST YOUR HUMOR LEVEL!

1. How many times a day do you laugh?

   a) I am a robot. Robots do not laugh.
   b) Several times an hour, including when I'm sleeping.
   c) I can't remember the last time I laughed.

d) Does that include giggles? I giggle all the time. Hee, hee, hee.
e) A lot. It feels good when I laugh.

2. Are you able to laugh at yourself?

   a) No way, buzz off!
   b) Only when I'm with good friends.
   c) Why? There's nothing funny about me.
   d) Yes, but it hurts on the inside.
   e) All the time; it relaxes me. I'm laughing now.

3. Is your family funny?

   a) My parents are utterly humorless.
   b) Only when they're drunk or high.
   c) My mom is hilarious when she gets angry.
   d) My dog cracks me up all the time.
   e) Actually, we laugh together pretty often.

4. How would you describe yourself?

   a) Class Clown
   b) Debbie Downer
   c) Laugh Riot
   d) Sour Puss
   e) Comic in Training

Find Your Funny

5. Do you laugh easily at other people's jokes?

    a) No. I am a robot. Robots do not laugh.
    b) Yes, 'cause it makes them happy.
    c) I try, but if the joke is really lame, it's hard to fake it.
    d) No, I don't think jokes are funny.
    e) Sure; it feels good to share the laughter.

6. What do you do for a lift when you're feeling down or overwhelmed?

    a) I eat a lot of candy, especially chocolate.
    b) I scream at my mom and blame her for the way I feel.
    c) I listen to zombie music for hours.
    d) I sleep a lot.
    e) I play video games and surf the web for funny videos.

7. Which of the following are funny?

    a) Rubber chicken
    b) Propeller hat
    c) Whoopee cushion
    d) Slipping on a banana peel
    e) All of the above

8. True or false: humor can be used to fix a flat tire.

   a) Only if your parents are members of AAA.
   b) Sure, if it's full of hot air.
   c) No way. Try a wrench, lug nuts and a jack.
   d) Beats me. My mom drives me everywhere.
   e) No, but it can lift you up sometimes.

9. Complete the sentence. The funny bone is...

   a) Connected to the thighbone.
   b) Made of Silly Putty.
   c) Non-existent in teachers and parents.
   d) A dense, porous, calcified connective tissue.
   e) Not really a bone, but a muscle that needs flexing.

10. Which of the following is your sharpest sense?

    a) I am a robot. I have no clue. STOP asking me!
    b) Definitely smell.
    c) Common sense is my best sense.
    d) Rapper 50 Cent?
    e) Let me guess...a sense of humor!

11. What do you think "Laughter is the best

medicine" means?

a) Laughter helps you. You don't need a prescription from the doctor.
b) It's healthier than a teaspoon of sugar. Sugar makes you fat.
c) When you laugh, you stop being so mad at stuff.
d) There's no co-pay?
e) If you laugh, you feel better even if you're sick or sad.

12. A good sense of humor is...

a) A gift from God or Santa.
b) Something you're born with–like flat feet.
c) Something to share with friends.
d) A skill like karaoke or riding a bike.
e) A way to make every day less stressful and more fun.

Scoring

Of the 12 questions, if you answered them all, give yourself a gold star.

If you answered questions 1, 3, 5, 7, 9, and 11 (a) or (b), give yourself a silver star.

If you answered questions 2,4,6,8,10, and 12 (c) (d) or (e), give yourself two gold stars, a stripe and a polka dot.

No matter what your score, you can always have more humor in your life.

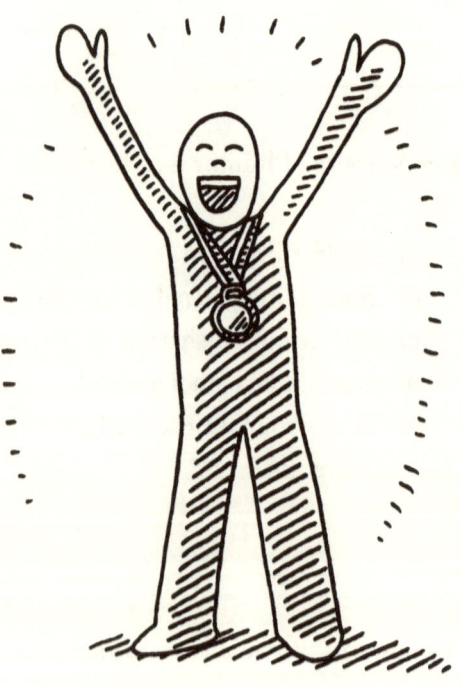

THREE
WHAT MAKES YOU LAUGH?

> "Life literally abounds in comedy if you just look around you."
> —Mel Brooks

Humor is subjective; it's a very individual thing. Ever notice how a joke may crack up a friend of yours, but not you? Sometimes it's even harder to get a group of people to agree on what's funny. Just ask a stand-up comic who's bombing!

Subjective: based on or influenced by personal feelings, tastes, or opinions.

There are several different genres of comedy and humor that will undoubtedly amuse you. Here are some you may recognize.

- **OBSERVATIONAL HUMOR**
  A very popular technique with stand-up comedians. Jerry Seinfeld is famous for it. His TV sitcom, *Seinfeld*, about "nothing" was really about everyday life–with some crazy characters and a little exaggeration added. If you've never seen *Seinfeld*, there's a terrible gap in your education! Go online and stream it!

- **PARODY/SPOOF**
  An imitation of the style of a particular genre with deliberate exaggeration for comic effect.

  Movie Examples: *Airplane, Blazing Saddles, Scary Movie Young Frankenstein,* and *Austin Powers.*

- **SLAPSTICK**
  Broad physical comedy based on gags – deliberately clumsy actions and silly events.

  Movie Examples: *Home Alone, The Pink Panther, National Lampoon's Vacation, Ace Ventura: Pet Detective The Mask* and *The Waterboy.*

- **SATIRE**
  Humor that relies upon irony, exaggeration or ridicule to expose and criticize people's stupidity or vices, particularly in the context of contemporary politics and authority figures.

  TV Examples: *Saturday Night Live*.

  Movie Examples: *Modern Times*, *Dr. Strangelove or: How I Learned to Stop Worrying and Love the Bomb*, and *MASH*.

- **FISH OUT OF WATER**
  The main character finds himself in a totally unfamiliar environment, one most unsuited to him. This incongruity drives the comedy.

  Movie Examples: *Big*, *Freaky Friday*, *Tootsie*, *Legally Blonde*, *My Cousin Vinny*, *Meet the Parents* and *Sister Act*.

- **ROMANTIC COMEDY**
  A light-hearted comedy that features the development of a love relationship.

  Movie Examples: *Roxanne*, *The Wedding Singer*, *Clueless*, *The Devil Wears Prada*, *Sleepless in Seattle* and *Legally Blonde*.

- **SCI-FI COMEDY**
  A comedy that uses the elements of traditional science fiction and/or addresses the supernatural.

  Movie Examples: *Ghostbusters, Beetlejuice, Sleeper* and *Men in Black*.

- **ACTION COMEDY**
  A comedy featuring one or more main characters who engage in witty dialogue between and during a prominently action-filled plot line. Lots of chases!

  Movie Examples: *Beverly Hills Ninja, Beverly Hills Cop* and *Men in Black*.

- **BLACK COMEDY**
  A comedy genre that makes light of serious subjects such as death or war.

  Movie Examples: *Dr. Strangelove or: How I Learned to Stop Worrying and Love the Bomb, Don't Tell Mom the Babysitter's Dead, Harvey, Raising Arizona* and *MASH*.

> "I like nonsense—it wakes up
> the brain cells."
> **– Theodor Seuss Geisel (Dr. Seuss)**

Comedy and humor—whether in literature, TV or film—often consist of basic ELEMENTS. Here are some of the more effective ones.

- **SURPRISE**

    An unexpected event. Aristotle's definition of humor: "something unexpected, the truth of which is recognized."

    One way surprise is used in humor is called a *paraprosdokian*. No kidding!

    Paraprosdokian: A figure of speech in which the latter part of a sentence or phrase is surprising or unexpected in a way that causes the reader or listener to reframe or reinterpret the first part. It is frequently used for humorous or dramatic effect, sometimes producing an anticlimax. For this reason, it is extremely popular among comedians and satirists.

    Example: "Before you criticize someone, walk a

mile in his shoes. That way, you'll be a mile away and he won't have any shoes." –Jack Handey

- **PUN and WORDPLAY**
  The witty exploitation of the meanings and ambiguities of words, especially in puns. You'll see a play on words, double-entendres and quips in funny dialogue and repartee.

A **PUN** is a joke exploiting the different possible meanings of a word or the fact that there are words that sound alike but have different meanings.

There are two types of puns: **Sound** and **Semantic**.

 *Semantic*: relating to meaning in language or logic.

Puns are based on **sound** play, on the way the word sounds. Here are some examples from PunOfTheDay.com.

> "He drove his expensive car into a tree and found out how the Mercedes bends."

"Need an ark to save two of every animal? I Noah guy."

Puns based on **semantics** play on word meanings. Here are some examples from PunOfTheDay.com.

"I'm reading a book about anti-gravity. It's impossible to put down."

"I'm glad I know sign language; it's pretty handy."

- **SET-UP**
  In a joke, it's the beginning.

  Example: *A woman hired a painter to paint her porch. After 30 minutes, the painter came to the door and said, "I'm done." The woman asked, "How did you get done so fast?"*

- **PUNCHLINE**
  The final phrase or sentence of a joke or story, providing the humor or some other crucial element like a delightful surprise.

  Example: *The painter said, "I'm a fast worker and by the way, it's a Ferrari not Porsche."*

All together now!
SET-UP + PUNCHLINE = JOKE

A woman hired a painter to paint her porch. After 30 minutes, the painter came to the door and said, "I'm done." The woman asked, "How did you get done so fast?" The painter said, "I'm a fast worker– and by the way, it's a Ferrari not a Porsche."

- **TIMING & RHYTHM**
The measured flow of words, phrases and events in the story. For comic effect,

1-2-3-PUNCH is a winner.

Three guys were stranded on a tropical island. One of them found a magic lamp and excitedly brought it to the others. He rubbed it. Out popped a Genie who said, "I'll grant each of you one wish." The first guy said, "I wish I was home with my family." Whoosh! He was home. The second guy said, "I sure wish I was home with my family, too." Whoosh! He was home, too. The third guy looked at the Genie and whined, "Man, I'm lonely here. I wish my friends were here." Whoosh! The two friends appeared back on the island.

- **EXAGGERATION**
  An overstatement; hyperbole. In comedy, over-emphasizing the negative or how bad something is dramatizes the situation.

- **IRONY**
  Using language that normally signifies the opposite; often uses sarcasm, paradox, incongruity of situation; a key element in satire.

  Example: In the movie *Tootsie*, a man (Dustin Hoffman) pretends to be a woman to get a part in a TV soap opera, then learns he can become a better man by "being" a woman.

- **INCONGRUITY**

Incongruity: Something that doesn't seem to fit in with or be appropriate to its context. Uses disparate elements.

Humor can be found in the combination of two ideas that don't normally go together. For instance, consider the seriousness of the political philosophy of Marxism and the wackiness of the comedy of the Marx Brothers.

This is called incongruity and it is a heavily used element in comedy. Watch for it. Don't know who the Marx Brothers are? Say it ain't so! You probably know Groucho Marx. He's the guy with the black mustache, bushy eyebrows, black glasses and a cigar.

You can buy plastic "Groucho glasses" with fake nose, mustache and eyebrows glued on.

Find Your Funny

Everyone should have a pair for formal occasions!

FOUR
HOW TO BE A HUMOR SPONGE

> "To succeed in life, you need three things: a wishbone, a backbone and a funny bone."
>
> – Reba McEntire

So, where's the funny? How can you find your funny?

There are strategies you can employ in your personal quest for a humor-rich life. Some of the ideas will appeal to you, some of them won't. Choose the ones you like and try those first. But don't stop there. At least *try* some of the ideas that, at first, may seem stupid or silly. Reach out of your comfort zone.

Find Your Funny

A sense of humor is learned, not inherited, but if your parents are a little goofy, you've got a head start! When we're around people who are funny and we see the humor in their lives, we begin to see it, too, and we get funnier. Laughter is contagious!

Here are some ideas for getting your sense of humor humming. Remember, making other people laugh is not as important as being able to amuse yourself and improve your own mood.

The first group of techniques is designed to get you thinking and seeing "funny," to get more humor and happiness in your life in a general way. They are arranged from the easiest, most low-risk, low-tension strategies to the slightly more risky and challenging ones. They go from the passive "just soaking it in" methods to the active "trying to get a laugh" methods. Have fun!

- **Expose Yourself!** (No! Not that way!)

    Expose yourself to ALL sorts of comedy.

    Watch funny movies, TV shows and comedians.

    Listen to comedy songs. Weird Al Yankovic is a comedian who writes and performs parodies of popular songs. His videos are popular on

YouTube. His website is linked on the "Comedy 411" page in the back of this book.

Create your own digital collection of comedy movies and albums.

YouTube has some of the funniest videos anywhere. Create a "Favorites" list with videos that make you laugh.

Make lists of funny books, movies, TV shows and comedians. Go to the library or online or to the Humor section of a neighborhood bookstore and look through the books, calendars and joke books.

- **SAY CHEESE! TAKE A PHOTO** when you see something funny. It can be a t-shirt, funny sign, dog, cat, cockatoo, anything that makes you laugh. Snap it, then enjoy again and again. Great for sharing, too.

- **Buy a joke-of-the-day calendar.**
  This is a positive way to start the day. A joke a day keeps the shrink away.

- **Visit comedy websites.**
  Check out the awesome list in "Resources" at the end of the book in Comedy 411!

- **Make a Jar-of-Jokes.**
  Take one out when you need a laugh. Simple. Easy. Fun.

- **What are your favorite funny video games?**
  Reminder: Don't limit yourself to just what's familiar to you. Explore different types and styles of comedy. Go ahead. Expose yourself!

- **Laugh at other people's jokes and attempts at humor.**
  It doesn't get much easier than this. Sometimes we're not very generous with our laughter. Remember the physical, psychological, and social benefits of laughter? It will make you feel better to laugh, it will make the other person feel better when you laugh, it will encourage other people to laugh with you, and it may make other people more likely to laugh at your jokes and attempts at humor.

- **Collect cartoons, jokes, comic strips, funny pictures, posters and stickers from the web, newspapers and magazines.**
  Put them everywhere you can think of—without getting arrested, grounded or suspended! Stick them on your notebooks, in your locker, on your mirror, on your bedroom door, anywhere they are highly visible to you.

  Change them often to keep the humor fresh.

Find Your Funny

- **There are sooo many websites for jokes, one-liners and slogans.**

  Print out the ones that make you laugh and put them up. This is a very low-risk way to share your humor with others. If others like them, that's great. If they don't like them, it's no big deal. This technique is a particularly good one if you're a visual person.

- **Memorize a few funny lines that help you keep things in perspective.**

  Use them when you're feeling down or stressed. Add some motivational ones, too. They might help you feel better about yourself or a prickly situation.

"Nothing in life is to be feared.
It is only to be understood."
– Marie Curie

"Everybody is ignorant…only on different subjects."
– Will Rogers

"It always seems impossible until it's done."
– Nelson Mandela

> "You can't laugh and be afraid
> at the same time – of anything.
> If you're laughing, I defy you
> to be afraid."
>
> **– Stephen Colbert**

Find Your Funny

> "The search for absurdity and unusual behavior (especially in oneself) can initiate healthy self-deprecating amusement. Exaggeration and comparison are good ways to begin to laugh at oneself. Even slight exaggeration can tweak your perception of something and take it from difficult to funny."
>
> – Mary Kay Morrison,
> *Using Humor to Maximize Living: Connecting with Humor*

 *Self-deprecating*: tending to belittle yourself or your achievements.

Remember to look for humor everywhere. Observe people. Notice the ordinary things that people do and say everyday that seem normal, but are just a little crazy when you stop and think about them. People are funny!

Barb Best and Joanne Jackal PhD

Find Your Funny

Top Ten Ways to Find your Funny

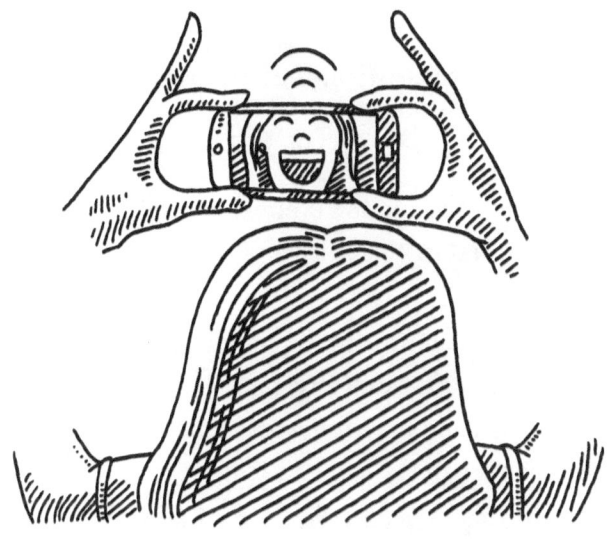

1. Expose yourself to all types and styles of humor.

2. Laugh at other people's jokes and attempts at humor.

3. Collect cartoons, jokes, comic strips, funny pictures and stickers and put them where you'll see them often.

4. Memorize funny and insightful lines and use them to help you keep things in perspective when

times are tough.

5. Hang out with funny people.

6. Wear t-shirts, buttons or hats that make you laugh.

7. Look for humor everywhere. Observe everyday life and its absurdity.

8. Gather funny props, clothing, costumes, hats, fake noses and any odd items that make you laugh and have fun with them.

9. Turn a difficult event into a funny "horror story."

10. Find some funny lines or jokes that suit your personality and share them.

Find Your Funny

You're so Funny!!! ☺ *Cool Comedy Pages* ☺

> Right now I'm having amnesia and déjà vu at the same time. I think I've forgotten this before.
> **–Steven Wright**

> Two cannibals are eating a clown. One says to the other: "Does this taste funny to you?"

> Whenever I feel blue, I start breathing again.
> **–L. Frank Baum**

When tempted to fight fire with fire, remember that the Fire Department usually uses water.

You do not need a parachute to skydive. You only need a parachute to skydive *twice*.

Everywhere is walking distance if you have the time.
–Steven Wright

Find Your Funny

> I got my hair highlighted, because I felt some strands were more important than others.
> **—Mitch Hedberg**

> I wonder how much deeper the ocean would be without sponges.
> **—Steven Wright**

> I went to buy some camouflage pants the other day, but couldn't find any.
> **—Tommy Cooper**

The last thing I want to do is hurt you. But it's on the list.

Nobody had to tell Jack to think outside the box.
–Barb Best

You can't have everything. Where would you put it?
–Steven Wright

> I was born to be a pessimist.
> My blood type is B negative.
> **—Will Ferrell**

> Respect the dead—they
> look up to you.
> **—Barb Best**

> I'm desperately trying to figure out
> why kamikaze pilots wore helmets.
> **—Dave Edison**

Barb Best and Joanne Jackal PhD

> Is a hippopotamus a hippopotamus or just a really cool opotamus?
> –Mitch Hedberg

> I've had a perfectly wonderful evening, but this wasn't it.
> –Groucho Marx

> Instant gratification takes too long!
> –Carrie Fisher

> I'm a hypochondriac. But I manage to control it with a placebo.
> **–Dennis Miller**

> A burrito is a sleeping bag for ground beef.
> **–Mitch Hedberg**

> I was the kid next-door's imaginary friend.
> **–Emo Philips**

> A day without sunshine is like, you know, night.
> **–Steve Martin**

> What's another word for "thesaurus?"
> **–Steven Wright**

> Borrow money from a pessimist—
> he won't expect it back.
> **–Oscar Wilde**

> On my sixteenth birthday, my parents tried to surprise me with a car, but they missed.
> **–Tom Cotter**

> Never moon a werewolf.
> **–Mike Binder**

> If a word in the dictionary was misspelled, how would we know?
> **–Steven Wright**

> If all the world's a stage, where is the audience sitting?
> —Steven Wright

> I'm a lousy cook—I burn sushi.
> —Joan Rivers

> If a book about failures doesn't sell, is it a success?
> —Jerry Seinfeld

> My ability to turn good news into anxiety is rivaled only by my ability to turn anxiety into chin acne.
> **–Tina Fey**

> It wasn't that no one asked me to the prom—it's that no one would tell me where it was.
> **–Rita Rudner**

> Procrastination isn't the problem; it's the solution. So procrastinate now; don't put it off.
> **–Ellen DeGeneres**

> While you can only be young once,
> you can always be immature.
> **–Dave Barry**

> The worst time to have a heart attack
> is during a game of "charades."
> **–Demetri Martin**

> Adults are always asking kids what they
> want to be when they grow up, because
> they are looking for ideas.
> **–Paula Poundstone**

FIVE
SHARING THE FUNNY

> "Laughter is the shortest distance between two people."
> – Victor Borge

Want more friends? Humor is a great way to connect with others socially!

There is a very social aspect to humor and laughter. According to Robert R. Provine in his book, *Laughter: A Scientific Investigation*, we laugh 30 times more often when we are with people than when we are alone.

Have you ever laughed with a group of friends until your sides hurt and you could hardly breathe? OMG, have you even felt like peeing your pants?

Then when you try to explain what was SO funny to someone who wasn't there, it just isn't funny. Well, really, it's true when they say, "You just had to be there." The pleasure and excitement of sharing hilarity with others makes it seem funnier and creates an important connection.

Funny is popular! We laugh more if we like people, or if we want them to like us. Both boys and girls list "a good sense of humor" as one of the top qualities desired in a girlfriend or boyfriend.

> "All you need in the world is loveand laughter. That's all anybody needs. To have love in one hand and laughter in the other."
> **– August Wilson**

Find Your Funny

Humorist and stress management expert Leigh Anne Jasheway offers these valuable points in her book, *Don't Get Mad, Get Funny!*

- Laughter helps you communicate more effectively.

- It makes you more likeable.

- It helps people trust you.

- It makes you more fun to be around.

- People tend to be less threatened by you.

You can become the funny friend that kids love to hang out with and enjoy!

Sharing is Caring

- Use humor to break the ice in an unfamiliar or uncomfortable situation. Try memorizing some jokes, telling a funny story, repeating a funny line from a popular movie, or using a cartoon voice or funny face (think Jim Carrey) to amuse friends.

- Join the fun in social media. Funny posts and tweets are shared many more times than any other message. Add your own funny comments or pictures.

- Lighten up and have more friends. People will be more comfortable around you if you relax and take yourself lightly. You have permission to be playful! Take a humorous approach to yourself and your flaws. Extend this attitude to your friends, and they will love you for it!

- Hang! An easy, low-risk way to get your humor juices flowing is to hang out with funny people. As comedians, after doing our "sets" in the comedy clubs, we would go to an all-night coffee shop. We would talk about ideas for routines and jokes, tease each other, and try to top each other with clever comebacks. It was almost as much fun as performing and great practice for thinking fast and funny.

- When we're with funny people, we become funnier. Their habit of looking for the humor in life rubs off.

- Be spontaneous. People often laugh at the unexpected, quirky things.

- Have a comedy marathon. Invite friends over

Find Your Funny

for a comedy party. Ask them to bring funny DVDs or comedy books. Watch funny videos on YouTube or take turns telling jokes. Planning this in advance adds to the fun as you anticipate the party.

- Get a funny script from a play, movie or TV show, act out a scene or two with a few friends, and video it. Movie and sitcom scripts are online. The great thing is, you don't have to be any good! Save the video to play back when you need a laugh or want to remember the fun of making it.

- Humor is helpful in defusing tense or angry situations. Even in the middle of a conflict, you can step back and see if there is any humor in the situation. This is hard, but it helps everyone get a better perspective.

Remember, being funny is all about being generous and giving.

> "If I can get you to laugh with me, you like me better, which makes you more open to my ideas."
> **–John Cleese**

Barb Best and Joanne Jackal PhD

> "What I value more than
> all things is good humor."
>
> –Thomas Jefferson

SIX
GOING THE EXTRA SMILE

> "Humor is not a trick, not jokes. Humor is a presence in the world, like grace, and shines on everyone."
>
> – Garrison Keillor

We've learned that laughter, humor and happiness have an extremely good impact on our physical, psychological and emotional health. Happy, optimistic people generally live longer and are healthier. Humor helps us cope with our problems. It allows us to put our problems in perspective and not take ourselves SO seriously.

More Ideas to Flex your Humor Muscle

- Gather funny props, clothing, costumes, hats, fake noses and any odd items that make you laugh. Use them to amuse yourself, your friends and your family. Studying for an English exam might be more fun while wearing a tiara and a feather boa. And you'll actually improve your memory. Brain research shows that our brains like novelty and that we remember information better when our emotions are involved. You might even carry a few of these items with you for spur-of-the-moment humor breaks.

- Notice a funny or really stressful incident, a "horror story." Stressful situations can be funny, especially if a series of mishaps occurs that builds to a conclusion. This is called "re-framing." Try exaggerating certain parts and practice telling it to others. You can work on your delivery as you retell it. Don't give it a big build-up the first few times you try it. This will help you save face if no one else thinks it's funny.

- Time for some jokes! Even if you don't think of yourself as a joke-telling type, give it a try. Go online and read jokes until you find a few that make you laugh and fit your personality. Jot them down and build a collection. Even if you never tell them to anyone else, you can brighten up your own mood by reading them yourself. Slip a couple in your backpack. You might need a laugh during the day.

- Joke Writing. Check out the book Jay Leno's *How To Be the Funniest Kid in the Whole Wide World (Or Just in Your Class)*. It's chock full of advice and jokes.

- Tell jokes. Start with people you know will be kind! Once you have practiced on them, branch out. You'll improve as you become more comfortable. Funny voices and accents can make a joke or story even funnier.

- Start a comedy club at school or with friends.

- You can find a funny monologue to perform. Video your one-person show. That way, there can be no confusion about who's the star!

- Write funny lyrics to the tune of a familiar or favorite song. Things are much funnier for some reason when they are put to music. Choose any person or topic to write about. You can even write about a problem you're struggling to solve.

- "My life is a sitcom!" Write a sitcom about the people and situations in your life. It doesn't have to be brilliant! It's just a way to help you get a quirky perspective on the people and problems in your life. If you hate writing, at least try imagining your life as a sitcom. Which actors would you cast as the various people in your life? Exaggerate your problems in a funny way. Emphasize the strange imperfections of your personality. See the humor in what you go through every day.

- Ever dream of being a stand-up comic? Why not write a routine? Watch comedians and copy the style of the ones that you relate to the best. But really the final product isn't that important. The important thing is that you get a new perspective on your life. All of us are so intensely wrapped up in our own struggles and problems that we lose perspective. We often take everything too seriously.

> "Although writing jokes is fun, telling them is even more fun."
>
> **– Jay Leno**

Find Your Funny

- Step back. See your life from a little bit of a distance. Admit that you have faults and laugh at them. You'll start to see that your shortcomings don't really matter all that much. Who knows, you may end up as a famous stand-up comic! Hey, don't forget us when you're famous!

- Join a laughter yoga class. It's a yoga discipline where students learn yoga breathing and laughter exercises. For 15-20 minutes, the class laughs without the aid of jokes, comedy props, or funny videos. Forced, artificial laughter often turns into genuine laughter.

Top Seven Ways to Find More of your Funny!

1. Read a script for a movie, play, or TV show and act out scenes with friends.

2. No one's around? Find a monologue.

3. Start a comedy club.

4. Invent funny lyrics to familiar or favorite songs.

5. Imagine yourself as the star of a sitcom about the people and situations in your life.

Find Your Funny

6. Write your own stand-up comedy routine.

7. Join a laughter yoga class.

SEVEN
LIGHTS...CAMERA... LAUGHTER

> "There is nothing in the world like making people laugh."
>
> –Carol Burnett

Guess what? You can learn to be more playful. The techniques and tools that actors and comedians use to create a range of emotions and characters are available to all of us. And they are fun. They can be particularly effective in conjuring up the comic spirit in our quest for a more light-hearted life.

Be observant of yourself and others. Actors are always

watching how people behave and interact; you need to do the same. Observe people in various emotional states. How does calm and confidant look? How do optimistic people sound? When you improvise, the interaction with others will probably make you funnier and help you think faster on your feet. So go ahead, act up!

Five Comedy Improv Exercises

1. **What's This Object?**
   Why, it's anything you want it to be. Take a simple object like a broomstick. Use your imagination... what else could it be? A telescope? A pool cue? A guitar? A tight rope?

   You get the idea!

2. **Mirror, Mirror**
   You'll need two people for this one. One of you is the Leader; the other is the Reflection. The Reflection will copy every movement that the Leader makes. There is no talking. This exercise helps you with concentration and observation. Caution: It can lead to unexpected hilarity.

3. **Freeze Tag**
   This classic game offers you an opportunity to develop and demonstrate your senses of physical

and visual humor. The amusing thing here is to time your tag so your friend is in a ridiculous looking position—the sillier the better.

4. **Charades**
   Charades is a fun game that can be tailored to any age level. The object of the game is to convey a word or phrase without using any verbal communication. Categories traditionally include Books, Movies, TV Shows, Songs and Quotations—but you can make up your own. How about Historical Figures, Pop Stars, Inventors, Entrepreneurs, Athletes, Fashion Designers?

   Much of the humor derives from the challenge of communicating nonverbally, the incorrect (often silly) guesses, and inside jokes.

5. **Exaggeration Circle**
   (improvencyclopedia.org)

   Everyone stands in a circle. One player makes a little gesture (with or without a sound). The next player copies the gesture but makes it bigger. Keep going until the last player takes the gesture to the extreme.

If you can find an improv class in your area, take it!

Find Your Funny

Improvisation will make you a better listener, help you develop confidence in front of others, improve your conversational skills, keep you focused on the present, and encourage you to think fast on your feet. Pretty cool!

Sometimes our problems are so serious that there's very little we can do to make things better. But other times, we just need a little positive shift in our attitude to make our lives happier. At those times, using humor will definitely help.

> "I have seen what a laugh can do. It can transform almost unbearable tears into something bearable, even hopeful."
>
> **–Bob Hope**

> "Laughter is a survival tool. It helps us de-stress, learn, cope, transcend, recharge, renew, hope, optimize, enjoy, create, meditate, digest, exercise, connect, engage, energize, oxygenate, release, persist and persevere."
>
> **–Christa Scalies**

> "Humor improves vision.
> Things always look better
> after a good laugh."
>
> **–Larry Wilde**

EIGHT
HUMOR & HAPPINESS

> "Humor is mankind's greatest blessing."
>
> – Mark Twain

Having a good sense of humor is an important part of being happy. What do we mean by happy anyway? In general, happiness is a positive emotional state that includes a feeling of well being, optimism, hopefulness and contentment. It's more than just a temporary good mood. It's more long lasting than that.

Scientists have even located the area of the brain that is active when we are happy. Renowned neuroscientist

Richard J. Davidson, PhD, discovered it's the **left prefrontal cortex**.

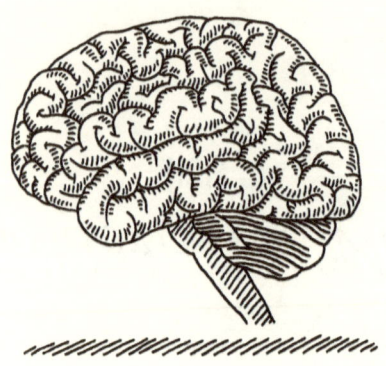

Happiness is important to our physical and mental health. When you're feeling good about something, your body feels energized, your muscles are relaxed and your breathing is deep and effective. You are more patient and generous with others and feel a greater sense of connection to them. Our attitudes affect how we feel physically and emotionally, how we see the world, and how we relate to other people.

An OPTIMISTIC attitude helps us bounce back when things go wrong. It helps us be more flexible and creative in our thinking, and may even help us live longer, happier lives.

OPTIMISM can decrease our anxiety and lower stress hormones. Ever feel so stressed you get stomachaches or headaches? When we're happier and more optimistic, we are less anxious and stressed.

Positive psychology researchers at the University of Pennsylvania developed happiness techniques that help people create more enjoyment in their lives. We've adapted these techniques to help you identify and develop more humor in your life.

- **"THREE THINGS"**

    At the end of the day, write down three things that made you smile or laugh. Why? It's pleasurable!

    ```
    1. My dog Buddy eating peanut
       butter

    2. When my sister tickled me
       on the bottom of my feet

    3. Watching Weird Al's new
       video
    ```

    It's also good for your brain, as it builds neural pathways that support positive thinking. The more you know about what is funny, the more you can create it.

- **"GRATITUDE" MESSAGE**

Think of someone who makes you laugh. Let them know via email, text or a phone call. Show your appreciation! They'll feel really good and will probably send even more "funny" your way.

> LOL! U cracked me up at lunch today . . . LMAO!

- **"RANDOM ACTS OF HUMOR"**

Give it some thought. How can you lighten up someone else's world with humor? Share your funny.

> "Voila"
>
> ```
> My sister who's dyslexic
> often gets embarrassed by
> mispronouncing words so I
> help her by saying them in
> a goofy foreign accent.
> This makes her laugh and
> also remember the word.
> ```

WAIT! Maybe you *don't* want to be happy. Nobody has the right to make you be happy if you *don't* want to be. It's up to you. So, if you *don't* want to be happy, knock yourself out!

Seven Easy Steps

1. **DON'T LAUGH**

    Refuse to see the humor in any situation. Take yourself way too seriously. Suck the life out of every room you enter. Don't stop until everyone feels your pain.

2. **BE NEGATIVE**

Have a negative attitude about everything. See only the bad in every situation. Be cynical. Make fun of people who are optimistic and cheerful.

Cynical: doubting or belittling of human nature or of the motives, goodness or sincerity of others

3. **ACT LIKE A VICTIM**

   Give up all control of your life. Feel like you don't have the power to change anything. Be passive.

4. **AVOID CHALLENGING YOURSELF**

   Don't try anything that is difficult or new. Not even a hard video game! Don't set goals or try to achieve anything except the absolute minimum necessary to get by.

5. **FOCUS ONLY ON YOURSELF**

   Put yourself and your needs front and center. Your mantra should be "Me, Me, Me!" Don't you dare care about anyone. Don't notice the world around you. And, whatever you do, don't participate in any of those suck-up groups trying to improve your school, better the community, clean up the environment, that sort of thing.

6. **SABOTAGE YOUR RELATIONSHIPS**

   This one is really important! If you're not careful, you'll end up with a lot of loving people in your life. This could cause happiness! Make sure all relationships are shallow or phony. If a friendship starts going well, ruin it in some way. Ditch it and run!

7. **HAVE NO FAITH OR VALUES**

   Don't be spiritual or religious. Don't have any values. Have no idea what you stand for or what's important in your life.

> "Laughter is the GPS system for the soul. Humor offers a revolutionary, yet simple, spiritual paradigm: If you can laugh at yourself, you can forgive yourself. And if you can forgive yourself, you can forgive others. Laughter heals. It grounds us in a place of hope."
>
> **– Rev. Susan Sparks,**
> *Laugh Your Way To Grace*

> "I realize that humor isn't for everyone. It's only for people who want to have fun, enjoy life, and feel alive."
>
> **–Anne Wilson Schaef**

 **SAT Word**

Sabotage: a deliberate action aimed at weakening another entity through subversion, obstruction, disruption or destruction.

How not to be ☺

Below are the seven steps for preventing ☺.

Put them up where you can see them and commit them to memory if you really want to be ☹.

SEVEN STEPS ☹

1. DON'T LAUGH
2. BE NEGATIVE
3. ACT LIKE A VICTIM
4. AVOID CHALLENGES
5. FOCUS ONLY ON YOURSELF
6. SABOTAGE RELATIONSHIPS
7. HAVE NO FAITH OR VALUES

NINE
GOOD HUMOR GONE BAD

> "There is a thin line that separates laughter and pain, comedy and tragedy, humor and hurt."
>
> –Erma Bombeck

Ouch! Sometimes humor is used to hurt people and that's definitely not funny. We can hurt people's feelings without meaning to, and that's bad enough. But when we do it on purpose, that's just cruel. Here are some humor YAYS and NAYS.

Yays

Make yourself the object of the humor without putting

yourself down. Self-deprecating humor is pretty safe, because it doesn't make other people feel threatened. People will appreciate your ability to take yourself lightly.

Make an awkward situation the subject of the humor. Again, no one feels threatened or picked on. Maybe that's why situation comedies are so popular. They create laughs by placing characters we can relate to into tricky situations and showing how they react.

Use humor to create a positive environment, to help people relax and feel better, not worse. Remember, one of the finest things that humor can do is to help people feel connected to each other.

Say you're sorry if you hurt someone's feelings when you're trying to be funny.

Maybe you think they're being too sensitive, but apologize anyway. Just do it! Sometimes it's hard to get people to agree on what's funny and what's not.

Nays

Don't attempt a joke when someone has just experienced a severe loss or trauma, like the death of a loved one.

Eventually, humor may help them, but they need time.

Let them take the lead.

Avoid making fun of anyone's ethnic, racial or religious group or sexual orientation. These are touchy topics even for professionals. When you use them in social situations, it can lead to a lot of hurt feelings and misunderstandings.

Never use humor to put people down. It is especially egregious, awful, immature, cruel, appalling and bad form to make fun of people who are younger or more vulnerable than you! Ridicule and sarcasm are very sharp tools that people use to express their anger, and hostility. Their use creates a negative environment and reverses all the benefits of humor and laughter that we're trying to create. A good rule to follow is to remember to respect the feelings of others.

 *Egregious:* Outstandingly bad; shocking.

Humor And Bullies

What's funny about bullies? Not much! And if you are being bullied or know someone who is, we strongly suggest that you use the resources in the back of this book to find some serious help. There is no shortage of advice and help on this difficult subject, so reach out and take it if you need it.

Our tips focus on ways to manage your behavior to avoid being bullied, to cope with bullying if it happens, and to check your own conduct regarding bullying.

Tips

- Taking yourself lightly and not being too serious and sensitive about yourself will make you less of a target. Bullies don't have as much fun if you don't get upset.

- Using your sense of humor can help you put the situation in perspective if you are being bullied. Obviously, if it is serious, on-going and abusive bullying, you must get help. But if you can step back from the situation and not overreact, you will be better able to cope with it. Someday you might even see some humor in it.

Find Your Funny

> "Comedy = Tragedy + Time."
>
> **–Carol Burnett**

- Never use humor to bully anyone. Have you ever made a joke at someone else's expense just to look cool? Ever make a nasty comment and then say, "Just kidding!" Ever mock someone because he or she was afraid?

- If you witness bullying, don't give bullies an audience or laugh at their behavior. Bullies love attention. You can easily become part of the problem if you support them by laughing at what they're saying or doing.

Our tips on bullying don't include using funny comeback lines. We don't recommend trying to respond to bullies in sarcastic or clever ways. Yes, it would be SO satisfying to have a devastatingly funny comeback line or two when bullied; however, in highly stressful situations, people rarely have the presence of mind to carry off humor. We only see that work successfully in movies and on scripted TV shows! Also, it gives the bully the attention he craves and can actually backfire by making him angrier and giving him more ammunition for further bullying.

> "Most comedy is based on getting a laugh at somebody else's expense. And I find that that's just a form of bullying in a major way. So I want to be an example that you can be funny and be kind, and make people laugh without hurting somebody else's feelings."
>
> –Ellen DeGeneres

 ***Devastating:*** highly destructive or damaging. **informal** extremely impressive, effective, or attractive

Gender Differences: He Laughed / She Laughed

This seems like a good time to bring up a very exciting topic: SEX! (Well, actually "gender.")

Have you noticed? Often, boys and girls find different kinds of things funny. Boys and girls have different life experiences, so it just makes sense that they would find different things funny. Of course, there are tremendous differences in what any two groups would consider funny. There are also lots of differences within groups regarding what's funny and what's not. But the battle of the sexes is always exciting, so here goes.

Stanford University psychiatrist Allan L. Reiss, MD, recruited 20 male and female college students. Inside an MRI scanner, the men and women looked at 70 cartoons flashed on a small overhead screen and rated them on a funniness scale. When the results came back, Reiss made an unexpected discovery: men and women process funny differently. The analytical region of women's brains was more active than the men's, suggesting women studied the cartoons more. When they found the cartoon amusing, the reward region of their brains lit up noticeably more than the guys'.

This is a fancy way of saying women appear to think a little more about whether they find something humorous. They don't necessarily expect to laugh, and so they enjoy it a lot more when the joke works for them. With men, apparently, it was more like, "Hey dude, a cartoon. Must be funny."

And here's some research that might help you avoid "humor misunderstandings" or soothe past hurts. Several studies have shown that "put-down" humor appeals more to men than women. Women generally see this kind of humor as hostile and are offended by it more often than men are. Women use self-deprecating humor more often, as well as stories and anecdotes. Men like to tease and razz and use mock hostility. Women often mistake the teasing and mock hostility for real feelings. Men often mistake women's mock self-deprecating humor as their real feelings. Women and men both tend to scoff at each other's form of humor.

Once we understand and accept each other's style of

humor, we can stop feeling hurt and have more fun. It takes patience and practice.

Try this.

Girls, remember it's nothing personal! It's just the way the guys connect and interact. The key is to relax and not take the put-down humor too seriously. It goes without saying, of course, that humor that becomes abusive is not funny, and no one has to put up with that. The same goes for humor that turns into sexual harassment. But as far as the regular razzing and teasing that guys tend to do, try to take it in stride. You might even try your hand at it. Practice some snappy comebacks. Listen to people who do it well and try to come up with your own lines that reflect your style and personality.

Guys, practice some witty humor that doesn't involve putting anyone down and add that to your repertoire. Be aware that not everyone likes being teased. Watch for negative reactions and knock it off if someone is getting irritated.

Also, remember, just because a girl is joking about her shortcomings doesn't mean she is weak or in need of therapy! Try using your own flaws as the basis of some humor and see how that goes. It's an especially good style around girls.

We can all use more humor and laughter in our lives. Research tells us that 62% of females mention a "good sense of humor" as a desirable quality in males, and that males are more interested in a woman who can laugh in their presence. If we learn to appreciate what the other half thinks is funny, we automatically double our chances for a laugh!

TEN

YOU'VE GOT TO BE KIDDING

Fun Facts about Laughter and Jokes

- There is an entire field dedicated to the physiological study of laughter. It's called *gelotology*.

- The average adult laughs 17 times a day.

- According to humor researcher and author Paul McGhee, PhD, "until the late 19th century, laughter was commonly considered detrimental to both physical and spiritual well-being – not to mention impolite and sinful."

- In Tanganyika (present-day Tanzania) in 1962, an isolated fit of laughter in a group of school girls grew to epidemic proportions. The laughter spread from one person to another, then spread to nearby communities. It was so severe that schools had to be temporarily closed. The laughter epidemic lasted for six months.

- Laughing 100 times is equal to ten minutes on the rowing machine or 15 minutes on an exercise bike. Laughing for 15 minutes can burn off about 52 calories. At that rate, you could laugh off about four pounds a year!

- Ever wonder why you can't tickle yourself? For tickling to tickle, there needs to be tension and surprise. You just can't fool yourself about it.

- We have much more conscious control of speech than we do of laughter. About half the people asked in one study by neuroscientist Robert R. Provine could not laugh on command.

- On September 9, 1950, at 7:00 p.m., on *The Hank McCune Show*, the first laugh track was used during a television sitcom to make up for the lack of a live audience. The rest is history!

- Dr. Madan Kataria, a physician from Mumbai, India, created Laughter Yoga. He and his wife,

Madhuri, founded an international movement with the mission of global health, happiness and world peace. And that's no joke.

- There are 5000 Laughter Clubs around the world with more than 250,000 members. There is even a World Laughter Day during which people on all five continents march and celebrate and laugh to promote world peace. The celebrations include dancing, music, food and laughter competitions.

- Mary Kay Morrison, the founder and director of Humor Quest, teaches educators how to use the positive energy of humor to promote balance and reduce stress. Through her research into cognitive learning, she promotes healthy humor and *humergy*, the vigorous, optimistic energy of humor.

- Dr. Richard Wiseman, a British psychologist, conducted an experiment to determine the world's funniest joke.

Here's the joke that was voted the world's funniest:

Two hunters are out in the woods when one of them falls to the ground. He doesn't seem to be breathing; his eyes are rolled back in his head. The other guy whips out his cell phone and calls the emergency services. He gasps to the operator: "My friend is dead! What can I do?" The operator, in a calm, soothing voice says: "Just take it easy. I can help. First, Let's make sure he's dead." There is a silence, and then a shot is heard. The guy's voice comes back on the line. He says: "Okay, now what?"

We find jokes funny for lots of different reasons; they sometimes make us feel superior to others, reduce the emotional impact of anxiety-provoking events, or surprise us because of some kind of incongruity. The winning joke achieves all three of these objectives.

Find Your Funny

- The Roman Emperor Elagabalus was known to employ a prototype of whoopee cushions at dinner parties. The modern version was reinvented in the 1920s by the JEM Rubber Co. of Toronto, Canada, by employees who were experimenting with scrap sheets of rubber.

- **Castigat ridendo mores** is a Latin phrase that generally means "one corrects customs by laughing at them," or "he corrects morals by ridicule." Some commentators suggest that the phrase embodies the essence of satire; in other words, the best way to change things is to point out their absurdity and laugh at them.

- *Gelotology* is not the study of hair gel.

- One of the funniest sitcom episodes in TV history was about death and the importance of humor in dealing with tragedy. Check out "Chuckles the Clown Bites the Dust" from *The Mary Tyler Moore Show*.

- Laughter tends to occur in short bursts of vowel-like sounds such as "ha-ha," "ho-ho," or "he-he," which are repeated every fifth of a second.

- Each "ha" of a laugh lasts about 1/15th of a second.

- Most studies indicate that women laugh more than men.

- We are born to laugh! Recent studies reveal that babies begin to laugh when they are as young as 17 days old.

- Around 200 BC, it is said that Greek philosopher, Chrysippus, died of laughter after giving his donkey wine and then watching it try to eat figs. (Don't try this at home.)

- In 1989, Danish audiologist Ole Bentzen, died of laughter while watching the movie *A Fish Called Wanda*. His heart was estimated to be beating between 250 and 500 beats per minute, causing him to die from cardiac arrest. (Don't worry–he had a previously undiagnosed heart problem.)

- In Thailand, Damnoen Saen-um, an ice cream truck driver, died while laughing hysterically in his sleep. (Not a bad way to go.)

- A University of California, San Francisco researcher identified 19 types of smiles and put them into two categories: polite "social" smiles that engage fewer muscles, and sincere "felt" smiles that use more muscles on both sides of the face.

- 13 muscles are used to smile, but 47 are required for frowning. You have to smile nearly a quarter of a million times to make one wrinkle.

- According to psychologist Tara Brach, the muscles used to make a smile actually send a bio-chemical message to our nervous system that it is safe to relax the flight or freeze response.

- University of Chicago studies show a great sense of humor can add eight years to your life.

- Do we laugh at funny things? Surprisingly, according to *Laughter: A Scientific Investigation* author Robert R. Provine, only 10%-20% of laughs are generated by anything resembling a joke. The other 80%-90% of laughter is due to dull non-witticisms like, "I'll see you guys later" and "It was nice meeting you, too." Provine suggests it has to do with the evolutionary development of laughter.

- Studies show that physical good looks, money, high IQ and higher levels of education have very little connection to happiness.

- Thoughts have physical properties. Every funny thought you have sends electrical signals through your brain.

- At Cancer Treatment Centers of America (CTCA), healers fight cancer using an integrative approach that offers supportive options, including laughter therapy, to help patients cope as they receive conventional cancer treatments. "Laughter Therapy" empowers people to use and enjoy laughter as a tool for healing.

- An anagram for funeral is "Real Fun." (Allen Klein, author of *The Healing Power of Humor*)

- When you laugh extremely vigorously, the lack of oxygen caused by the epiglottis blocking your windpipe can activate your tear ducts and make you cry.

- Nitrous oxide–commonly known as laughing gas–shows promise in alleviating severe depression. In 2014, a research team from Washington University School of Medicine in St. Louis, MO, reported findings of their proof-of-concept study into the effects of laughing gas on severe, treatment-resistant depression in the journal *Biological Psychiatry*.

Find Your Funny

- Rev. Susan Sparks is the only professional female comedian in the country with a pulpit. She is the senior pastor of the historic Madison Avenue Baptist Church in New York City.

- Rats love to be tickled. Bowling Green University psychology professor Jaak Panksepp has a video on YouTube that demonstrates this!

- Chimps tickle each other and even laugh when another chimp pretends to tickle them.

- Deaf people laugh without hearing.

- The definition of the fun word "felicific" is "relating to or promoting increased happiness." It is from Latin **felicificus**, from **felix felic- 'happy.'** Say that five times!

- In every episode of the TV sitcom *Seinfeld*, there is an image of Superman displayed somewhere on the set.

- According to humor researchers, the most effective (funniest) animal word to use in a joke is... (the envelope, please) DUCK!

- Funny words include: monkey, pickle, poppycock, squeegee, cheese, rump, kitten and underwear.

- Studies indicate that the perfect length for a joke is...(drumroll) 100 words.

"Ever stop to think, and forget to start again?"
—A.A. Milne

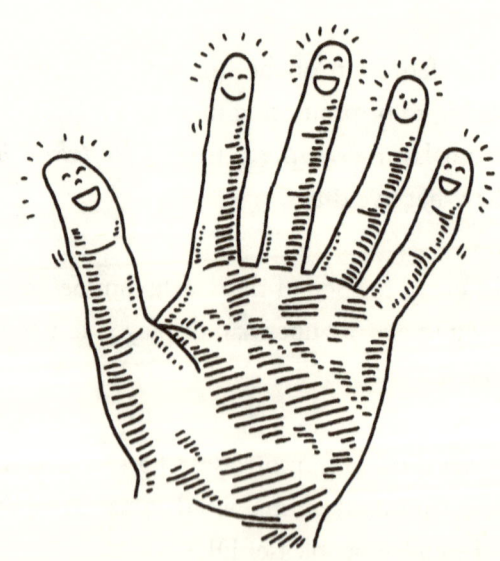

RESOURCES
COMEDY 411

Funny Stuff Is Out There! Find Your Funny!

Multimedia mirth abounds! Here's a list of funny websites, TV shows, movies, sketches and songs.

- Animal Planet
- Comedy Central
- Disney
- Funny or Die
- Hulu
- Kids 'N Comedy
- Nickelodeon

- Pun of the Day
- Saturday Night Live
- Shel Silverstein
- The Cartoon Network
- TVland
- Weird Al
- YouTube

Find Your Funny

COMEDY MOVIES

A Fish Called Wanda
Ace Ventura Pet Detective
Airplane!
All of Me
American Pie 2
Anchorman
Austin Powers
Beethoven
Beetlejuice
Beverly Hills Cop
Beverly Hills Ninja
Big
Billy Madison
Blazing Saddles
Broadway Danny Rose
Caddyshack
Christmas With the Cranks
Clueless
Coming to America
Diary of a Wimpy Kid
Don't Tell Mom the Babysitter's Dead
Dr. Strangelove
Duck Soup
Election
Elf
Father of the Bride
Ferris Bueller's Day Off
Freaky Friday
Ghostbusters
Hairspray
Harvey
Happy, Texas
Home Alone
Legally Blonde
Liar Liar

Little Miss Sunshine
Mean Girls
Meet the Parents
Men In Black
Modern Times
Monty Python's Life of Brian
Monty Python and the Holy Grail
Mr. Mom
Mrs. Doubtfire
My Cousin Vinny
Napoleon Dynamite
National Lampoon's Animal House
National Lampoon's Vacation
Nick and Norah's Infinite Playlist
The Parent Trap
Raising Arizona
Ratatouille
Revenge of the Nerds
Roxanne
Scary Movie
School of Rock
Scott Pilgrim vs. The World
Sister Act
Sleeper
Sleepless In Seattle
The Devil Wears Prada
The Jerk
The Mask
The Nutty Professor
The Pink Panther
The Princess Bride
The Three Amigos
The Waterboy
The Wedding Singer
This Is My Life
Tootsie
Toy Story
Trains, Planes & Automobiles
Up
Wayne's World
Who Framed Roger Rabbit?
Young Frankenstein
Zelig

What Does Laughter Look Like?

RESOURCES
TRAGEDY 411

When nothing seems funny...

You feel really bad. Dark. Desperate. You need to talk to someone.

HELP is on the way!

In addition to the usual suspects—parents, family members, friends, teachers and spiritual advisors—here are some EMERGENCY CONTACTS.

Hotlines

- **National Suicide Hotline**
  1-800-SUICIDE (784-2433)

- **National Suicide Prevention Lifeline**
  1-800-273- TALK (8255)
  Both toll-free, 24-hour, confidential hotlines that connect you to a trained counselor at the nearest crisis center.

- **Safe Place**
  1-888-290-7233
  Project Safe Place provides access to immediate help and supportive resources for young people in crisis through a network of qualified agencies, trained volunteers and businesses in 32 states. Call the hotline to find out if the program operates in your state or look online.

- **The Trevor Project**
  866-4-U-TREVOR
  The Trevor Project operates the only nationwide, around-the-clock crisis and suicide prevention helpline for lesbian, gay, bisexual, transgender and questioning (LGBTQ) youth. The Trevor Helpline is available as a resource to parents, family members and friends of young people as well.

MORE HELP! GO ONLINE

- **Suicide Prevention Lifeline**
  www.suicidepreventionlifeline.org
  The website for this 24-hour, confidential hotline offers details about how to call if you need help, how to identify suicide warning signs, and information for anyone experiencing mental distress.

- **CTL Crisis Text Line**
  www.CrisisTextLine.org
  Free and confidential support 24/7. Just text "HOTLINE" to 741741.

- **Giggle On**
  www.giggleon.com
  Christa Scalies, suicide prevention advocate and Author of *Suicide Sucks: Move through the Pain of Suicide Loss and Learn to Laugh Again*, offers valuable advice to those suffering from depression and/or a loss from suicide.

- **The Jed Foundation**
  www.jedfoundation.org
  The Jed Foundation works to reduce the stigma students feel about having or seeking treatment for emotional problems. It provides safe, accessible resources for students to help themselves or a friend.

- **The Cartoon Network–Stop The Bullying**
  www.cartoonnetwork.com/promos/stopbullying/index.html
  Entertainment site has excellent information and advice on bullying.

- **National Alliance on Mental Illness (NAMI)**
  www.nami.org
  A grassroots organization for people with mental illness and their families, NAMI has affiliates in every state and in more than 1,100 local communities across the country.

- **The Jason Foundation, Inc**
  www.jasonfoundation.com
  The Jason Foundation provides information, education programs and help in the fight against the "silent epidemic" of youth suicide.

- **Depressed Teens**
  www.thebalancedmind.org/flipswitch
  This website provides valuable information/educational resources for teenagers, their parents and educators to understand the signs and symptoms of teenage depression and get help when needed.

- **Al-Anon/Alateen**
  www.al-anon.alateen.org
  Al-Anon is a self-help group for people who are concerned about a friend or family member who is having trouble with alcohol or drugs. They provide practical help and support in how to deal with your friend or loved one.

ABOUT THE AUTHORS

Barb Best is an Erma Bombeck Global Humor Award winning writer. Her comedy material has been performed by Joan Rivers and her essays and light verse have been published in numerous print and digital publications. Barb's fun blog appears at BarbBest.com and was named one of the "Top 100 Humor Blogs on the Planet." Be sure to boost your feel-good hormones by treating yourself to Barb's latest book *The Misery Manifesto: A Self-Help Parody for the Self-Absorbed*. She feels your pain.

Joanne Jackal, PhD is a psychotherapist with more than twenty-five years experience treating children, adolescents and young adults for behavioral health and substance abuse problems. Her dynamic therapeutic approach utilizes elements of positive psychology, mindfulness, and cognitive therapy and is informed by an early career in New York City as a stand-up comedienne. "Who says therapy can't be fun?" is her mantra. "Helping people generate humor and laughter in the face of life's difficulties is one of the most important services I can provide."

ACKNOWLEDGMENTS

The authors share a deep commitment to serve children by inspiring them to lead happier, healthier, more humor rich lives.

Much thanks goes to the many smart and savvy folks who shared their feedback with us on various drafts of *Find Your Funny: The Survival Guide*.

We appreciate you supporting us in creating this helpful, accessible and fun book. We are particularly thankful that we didn't have to bribe or beg you for the amazing blurbs.

Mucho Gracias to Amy, Kai, Min and Kit Hannum—key participants in our principal focus group, Mindy Hoffbauer, editor at Write Angle Consulting, AATH (The Association of Applied Therapeutic Humor) and The Humor Academy, humor advocates Judy Oliverio, Linda Garner, Masako Kusakari, Amy Robbins, Jeunesse Pearson, Roberta Gold, and Barbara Grapstein.

But that's not all! Special thanks to authors Larry Wilde, Jim Winter, Sue Stephenson, Mary Kay Morrison, Christa Scalies and Suzanne Raga.

Last but not least, we'd like to thank our inner children without whose humor and resilience we would not be here today.

"We like you! We really like you!"

www.ingramcontent.com/pod-product-compliance
Lightning Source LLC
Chambersburg PA
CBHW030329080526
44584CB00012B/784